*The Hidden Language
of Symbolism*

By Annie Besant

Copyright © 2021 Lamp of Trismegistus. All rights reserved. No part of this publication may be reproduced or transmitted in any form or by any means, electronic or mechanical, including photocopying, recording, or by any information storage and retrieval system, without permission in writing from Lamp of Trismegistus. Reviewers may quote brief passages.

ISBN: 978-1-63118-585-4

Esoteric Classics

Other Books in this Series and Related Titles

Aurora of the Philosophers by Paracelsus (978-1-63118-507-6)

Clairvoyance and Psychic Abilities by A Besant &c (978-1-63118-403-1)

The Feminine Occult by various authors (978-1-63118-711-7)

Rosicrucian Rules, Secret Signs, Codes and Symbols by various (978-1-63118-488-8)

An Outline of Theosophy by C W Leadbeater (978-1-63118-452-9)

Paracelsus, the Four Elements and Their Spirits by M P Hall (978-1-63118-400-0)

Essays on Ancient Magic by Helena P Blavatsky (978-1-63118-535-9)

Essays on the Esoteric Tradition of Karma by A Besant &c (978-1-63118-426-0)

The Use of Evil by Annie Besant (978-1-63118-532-8)

Occult Arts by William Q. Judge (978-1-63118-559-5)

The Alchemical Catechism of Paracelsus by Paracelsus (978-1-63118-513-7)

Alchemy in the Nineteenth Century by Helena P Blavatsky (978-1-63118-446-8)

Qabbalistic Teachings and the Tree of Life by M P Hall (978-1-63118-482-6)

The Historic, Mythic and Mystic Christ by Annie Besant (978–1–63118–533–5)

The Hidden Mysteries of Christianity by Annie Besant (978–1–63118–534–2)

The Brotherhood of Religions by Annie Besant (978–1–63118–563–2)

Kali the Mother by Sister Nivedita (978-1-63118-558-8)

Arcane Formulas or Mental Alchemy by W W Atkinson (978-1-63118-459-8)

The Machinery of the Mind by Dion Fortune (978-1-63118-451-2)

Vision of the Spirit by C. Jinarajadasa (978-1-63118-560-1)

The Leadbeater Reader: A Selection of Occult Essays (978-1-63118-483-3)

Audio versions are also available on Audible, Amazon and Apple

Other Books in this Series and Related Titles

Eastern Magic & Western Spiritualism by Henry S Olcott (978–1–63118–584–7)

Spiritual Progress and Practical Occultism by H P Blavatsky (978–1–63118–583–0)

Memory and Consciousness by Besant & Blavatsky (978–1–63118–582–3)

The Origin of Evil by Helena P Blavatsky (978–1–63118–581–6)

The Camp of Philosophy: Studies in Alchemy by Bloomfield (978–1–63118–580–9)

The Testaments of the Twelve Patriarchs (978–1–63118–579–3)

Occult or Exact Science? by Helena P Blavatsky (978–1–63118–578–6)

Occultism, Semi-Occultism & Pseudo Occultism by A Besant (978–1–63118–577–9)

The Fourth-Gospel and Synoptical Problem by G R S Mead (978–1–63118–576–2)

On the Bhagavad-Gita by T Subba Row &c (978–1–63118–575–5)

What Theosophy Does for Us by C W Leadbeater (978–1–63118–574–8)

Spiritual Life for Man by Annie Besant (978–1–63118–573–1)

The Mysteries by Annie Besant (978–1–63118–572–4)

Fundamental Ideas of Theosophy by Bhagwan Das (978–1–63118–571–7)

Dreams: What They Are and Caused by C W Leadbeater (978–1–63118–570–0)

Communication Between Different Worlds by Annie Besant (978–1–63118–569–4)

Animism, Magic and the Omnipotence of Thought by S Freud (978–1–63118–568–7)

Buddhism by F Otto Schrader (978–1–63118–567–0)

Death by W W Westcott (978–1–63118–566–3)

The Religion of Theosophy by Bhagwan Das (978–1–63118–565–6)

The Spirit of Zoroastrianism by Henry S Olcott (978–1–63118–564–9)

Audio versions are also available on Audible, Amazon and Apple

Table of Contents

Introduction...7

Symbolism...9

Occultism is not the acquirement of powers, whether psychic or intellectual, though both are its servants. Neither is occultism the pursuit of happiness, as men understand the word; for the first step is sacrifice, the second, renunciation. Occultism is the science of life, the art of living.

INTRODUCTION

The word "esoteric" can be difficult to define. Esotericism in general can be seen less as a system of beliefs and more as a category, which encompasses numerous, different systems of beliefs. It's a bit of juxtaposition, since the word "esoteric" indicates something that few people know about, while the term itself broadly covers numerous philosophies, practices, areas of study and belief systems.

In a greater sense, Esotericism acts as a storehouse for secret knowledge, which is often considered ancient (by *tradition, if not by fact),* passed down from generation to generation, in private. At various times in history, simply possessing the knowledge of some of these subjects, was considered illegal and a jailable offence, if discovered. This usually included such general topics as Alchemy, Pharmacology, Qabalah, Hermeticism, Occultism, Ceremonial Magic, Astrology, Divination, Rosicrucianism and so on. Collectively, these areas of study were often referred to as the esoteric sciences.

Sometimes, the outer garment of a subject isn't esoteric, while what is hidden beneath it, is. As an example, Freemasonry isn't necessarily esoteric by nature (at *least not anymore),* but certain signs, passwords and handshakes given to the candidate during their initiation, are in fact, esoteric, in the sense that they are hidden from the general public.

Today, in the twenty-first century, such topics are readily available at bookstores across the country, and numerous mainsteam publishers offer beginners guides and coffee-table volumes on many of these subjects, intended for mass appeal. Books like *"The Secret"* have turned previously arcane topics into household knowledge. All that being the case, however, it isn't to say that there still aren't buried secrets to uncover, ancient wisdom being ignored and forgotten mysteries to be explored. In fact, it is often that we are only able to further our own studies by standing on the shoulders of these disappearing giants.

Lamp of Trismegistus is doing its part to help preserve humanity's esoteric history by making some of these classics available to those students who are seeking to unearth the knowledge of these ancient colossi.

So, be sure to check other titles from our *Esoteric Classics* series, as well as our *Occult Fiction, Theosophical Classics, Foundations of Freemasonry Series, Supernatural Fiction, Paranormal Research Series, Studies in Buddhism* and our *Christian Apocrypha Series.* You can also download the audio versions of most of these titles from Amazon, Apple or Audible, for learning on the go.

SYMBOLISM

Symbolism in religions may be called a common language. By this it is meant that certain external forms are taken, which, presented to the view of anyone versed in the forms, convey to the mind of that person a definite idea; just as, for instance, you may have an ideographic language which is read by each person into his own tongue; just as you may have numbers in arithmetic, each number carrying some idea, but if the number be put into spoken word, the word will differ according to the language which is employed. So, in all ages have men who have studied religions had a common language by which they could communicate with each other; so that no matter what might be the country of the person, no matter what might be the particular religion that exoterically surrounded him, when he came across the symbol, he recognized its meaning, and so had knowledge conveyed to him by his fellow Initiates, which to him was as definite and as certain as though it had been conveyed in his own particular language of words. Now of the underlying unity of religions there can be no greater proof than the identity of religious symbols. When you find within a Hindu temple the same symbols as you find in far-off ruins in Western lands; when you find the same symbol that is in the temple and in the Western ruins reproduced in the modern Christian cathedral or church; when you find in Asia, in America, in Europe and in many of the islands of the Pacific Ocean, just the same symbol reappearing; then you may know that the people who made the symbol held the same notion, used the same means to convey it, knew the same truth, and worshipped the same idea. And in this fashion, the study of symbolism may constantly enable us to gain from the past knowledge that has slipped away in the present. Thus we may know some great truth which conveys sustenance to our own thinking, and taking up some ancient Scripture, we may recognize under the garb of symbol, the truth which in some other fashion we have received. So taking the ancient books, which were written by great Sages, by Divine Instructors, we may find that they have hidden in these books secrets of spiritual knowledge, and that they have done it in order that the secrets might be preserved amongst all the changes and chances of life; and that when a man has reached a certain stage of spiritual evolution, there might be here ready to his hand knowledge that he might acquire. Thus what has been carried through ages of darkness may once again appear for the enlightening of the world. Inasmuch as today we are in a cycle of darkness, as we are living in that Kali Yuga, during which spirituality is at its lowest ebb, and inasmuch as this period is characterized by the triumphs of the powers of darkness and the blinding of the insight of man which in happier ages is clear and distinct, symbolism is to us of deepest moment. For when this cycle was approaching, it became necessary that the Sages should hide under symbol and under garb of outer fables those truths which were to be preserved for generations to come - not only in what we call ordinary symbolism or outer form, but also in allegory, in fable, in that which is regarded as myth, and in that which is used as ceremony. In all these things there is the heart of spiritual truth, and from time to time, someone arises who is able to see the truth underneath the outer symbol of fable or ceremony; and so bringing out the truth from the symbol, is able to strengthen man's belief in spiritual realities, and reassert in the midst of darkness the light of a happier time. For not only does symbol carry on truth from age to age, but it also acts as a constant witness for the existence of the truth. Sometimes it may be meant to hide it, but at other times it is meant that the hidden truth shall be brought out, so that the bringing out may re-establish man's belief in truth. The special work that is being done today by the Theosophical Society is done at the will of those Divine Instructors who devised the symbols and gave them in charge to the various religions of the world. So that from time to time what is to be done, and is being done today, is that when truth has been lost to the majority and when belief in it has largely disappeared, someone taking hold of the symbol shall explain it; then the reasonableness of the explanation recommends itself to the minds of men, and they feel the evidence of the existence of truth, because it is brought out, as it were, from its hidden recesses; then faith grows up again, and belief is once more able to lift up its head, because the unveiling justifies the reality of the symbol and they recognize the inner truth, and so become convinced of the light which was hidden, and which by the opening, as it were, of the lantern is once more revealed to the world. So that symbolism has this value of not only carrying on the truth, and of giving it to those who are wise, but also of impressing on the outer world the persistent reality of the spiritual truth; and it is the knowledge of this which makes some of us lay stress on the preservation of ceremonies, even when they are not understood. I know that in the minds of some, this seems folly and superstition; I know that in the minds of some, this seems to be raising an obstacle in the way of progress. They only see the ceremony from the standpoint of the obstacle; they do not realize the value that within that seeming obstacle may be enshrined. Sometimes there may be an ancient monument which tells of the past history of the people. You want to carry a railway through it, and you will say that it is very important that the railway should be a straight line between two points, and that it is far better to sweep away the ancient monument which has become an obstruction, and to allow the people to have the practical advantage of saving ten minutes of time, which will be lost if the railway goes round the monument. Instead of pulling it down and destroying it, it may sometimes be wiser to waste ten minutes' time - when so much time is wasted - than to destroy the records of an event that otherwise might pass without record out of the minds of men. So if the ceremonies, whose meaning even has been lost - lost for the present from the eyes of ordinary men, but not lost from the knowledge of spiritual Sages, and not lost in their future power, when once more the truth that they hide is revealed - if the ceremonies of Hinduism had been entirely swept out of India, where should we find the arguments for the reaffirmation of spiritual truth to the Indian people? But inasmuch as the ceremonies have remained and inasmuch as the symbols still exist, then, coming with knowledge, we can justify the ancient teaching even by these preserved symbols, and so can reach the hearts and minds of the people in a way that would be utterly impossible if the symbols had disappeared.

Now as an illustration, let me begin with one symbol which is universal and found in every religion, although in different religions differing very slightly in the shape in which it appears - I mean the famous symbol of the Cross, largely identified today in the modern world with a very modern religion, largely identified probably in the minds of many of you with that religion. It is none the less the most ancient of all the symbols, and has come down to us from a time lost to Western thought in obscurity. No matter how deeply you dig into the crust of the earth; no matter how ancient the ruins of the city that, by such digging, you may unbury; no matter whether you dig into that crust in America, in Europe, in Asia, and in Africa; everywhere you will find the Cross. There are places in Europe that have been unburied by modern investigation, places that are covered over with the ruins of civilizations which had absolutely disappeared from the surface of the earth long before the civilization of the Roman Empire was dreamed of - a civilization that endured for centuries and then fell into ruin.

Passing back over the millenniums and digging down through those ruins that tell of its decay, down through them all into still older ruins of a civilization that has left no trace, save in these deep buried records; even there you shall find a Cross marked on pottery that has long outlasted the very bones of thy people that made it; for the pottery, found beside little heaps of dust that vanish when the tomb is opened, has graven on it the symbol of the Cross, and buried by the side of the dead conveys its own sacred signification. Go back as far as you will into the antiquities of this - the most ancient of all lands so far as the Fifth Race of man is concerned - there is no place where you will not find this symbol; in the most ancient of the Scriptures you will find the Cross, representing, in later times, the circle of the horizon, representing farther back the form of Vishnu, which is Time. The circle symbolizes Time unending, and within it a Cross on which lie all Gods, all Rishis, all Suns and all Stars, everything which is in the manifested universe. Go farther back, before the Fifth Race is born - back into those times of which no record remains, save in the hands of the Initiates themselves - here and there is a rock of which they only can explain the meaning, and on these rocks, deep graven, there still is found the figure of the Cross. Go back to the Fourth Race of men, swallowed up by a mighty catastrophe, from which only the seed came over from which the Fifth Race was to spring; even there you will find the same symbol, sacred to the Fourth Race as it has been ever sacred to the Fifth. So that we may take it as a universal symbol, one that we cannot permit one of the latest and most modern of religions to usurp as though it belonged only to it. For it is a symbol often stamped on the breast of the Initiates, sacred to religion in its deepest recesses, and not the private property of one of the most modern and exoteric of faiths. Take then the Cross - what is it fundamentally? It was in the circle always in the oldest records; in later times the circle has fallen away from it, and the Cross, losing the circle, became degraded from its loftiest significance. Always the symbol has its highest meaning in the Spirit; and from the spiritual sphere it comes downward into outer manifestation and finds a second explanation in the stars which are the outer forms of the great Intelligences, by which the Kosmos moves; and then lower still it falls, until it comes down to man, and then it becomes more degraded in its latest phallic signification, polluted by the impure thoughts that flow to it from the mind in man. Take then the circle, and in its earliest significance it stands for that Boundless Existence which, coming into manifestation, circumscribes Itself. First, we have been taught of a circle of light bounded by darkness which has no limit; and the circle of light is the beginning of the manifested Kosmos. Thus we found in studying light that first we had light without form, and then later form came as the visible side of the manifestation; and the circle in its earliest significance means manifestation, therefore limitation, the beginning of things. The Cross which, as the next stage, divides it is that fire which, flashing from the centre outwards, makes two diameters, gives active life within this circle of the universe, and makes possible the evolution which from the centre is gradually to proceed. At first, one line of the Cross is the line drawn in both directions by the light of the Logos from the centre outwards to the circumference - that light of the Logos that I spoke of in the second lecture, as shining out from the dual Logos, from that which we saw as Fire and Water, that which is Spirit-Matter, shining out from the centre which is the unmanifested Logos; this, passing outwards to the circumference, divides the circle first into two and then into four. It is this line of light starting from the point, passing outwards in the four directions, that traces the first Cross in manifestation, the symbol of the division into Spirit and Matter. Then coming down a little further and recognizing this division of Spirit and Matter, there is the generation of the Kosmos, which is symbolized by the revolution of the Cross, so that the Cross is no longer two straight lines, but to each arm of the Cross there is attached a part of the circle of manifestation, and you get the ancient Svastika, which gives not only the idea of division, but also the idea of revolution. In the Svastika, with the limbs turned, there is a suggestion of the circle as well as of the Cross, but no longer of the circle set and steady, but of the circle revolving, having therefore become a generating force of life. Closely united with this is the symbolism of the fire-sticks; here you have a socket which stands for the circle, and the upright stick which is made to revolve by a cord (thus forming a Cross) which, turning it round and round in the socket, generates fire, which is sacred, so giving birth to Agni the Fire-God, as the sign of that Life by which only the universe can appear. Thus you have not only the circle, not only the upright stick which represents half the Cross, but also the string which completes the Cross and causes revolution. There is the completed image of the second Logos by whose division further manifestation becomes possible. Then with the revolution, then with the heat which is generated - to which you may remember I drew your attention, as the result of this action of fire - when the mere radiance of light passes into fire, it is then you get the birth of the Fire-God, without whose generating influence no further manifestation may come. Then you can trace it downwards and downwards, through slight changes in the outer form, until you find it as everywhere symbolical of the God, of the God in manifestation, an essentially creative and productive power in the universe in its highest sense; in its highest sense the God that generates the Kosmos. In its lowest sense it is the representative of the reproductive organ, that too often gives rise to forms of esoteric worship which have become a degradation. The blinded eye of the Materialist reads but the phallic meaning, and reads into it his own impure signification; whereas that is the lowest point of materiality, while the highest is that which begins in the Logos itself, manifesting itself in the world of form. Thus tracing the Cross we find it in ancient sculptures in the hands of the Gods, constantly present, shaped slightly differently according to the type adopted by the people in their religion. There again there is another use of this symbolical language, for, according to the particular shape the symbol has assumed, we are able to judge of the stage to which the religion of that people has evolved. Take, for instance, the Egyptian religion; there you will find the Cross and the circle changed in appearance. The Cross is no longer the Cross which is traced on the circle of Time, with its two arms of equal length. It has become the letter **T** with one arm below the other, and instead of being within the circle of Time, the circle has gone outside it and rests on the top of the Tau. The circle is no longer Time, it stands for the female principle. In the hands of the Gods you may see it traced in the frescoes on the pyramids; you will find it there held as a symbol of human life; and when the mummy is lying prone and the time comes for the Soul to revivify it, then the God comes forward with this Tau and circle in his hand, the Cross of Life, and he touches with the lips of the mummy and thus restores the Soul and brings the body to resurrection, to the possibility of renewed life. Instead of taking it in the later Egyptian religion, where it has fallen from its highest significance, let us take it in the hand of one of the Hindu Gods, and you will find that a subtler and a more beautiful significance may be drawn from it. Take the image of Shiva, Maha-deva, as you will find Him sometimes represented in the temples - represented as the Maha-Yogi, the great Ascetic, who by Tapas burned up everything that was of the lower nature and remained as Fire only; everything else having disappeared. The Maha-Yogi holds in His uplifted hand a cord - a cord that assumes an oval shape and not a circle - and He holds that in His uplifted hand, between the thumb and the fingers; and you will see that the oval rises above the hand, and that the hand makes the figure of the Cross on which this oval is supported. What can be the meaning in the hand of the great Yogi, the patron of all ascetics, what can be the meaning of this symbol, which in more modern literature has been taken as the productive symbol, the symbol of life? Has not the Yogi turned aside from this creative activity, for he is often symbolized by the virgin Kumara, who has refused to create and who has nought to do with physical manifestation? The symbol has a loftier meaning. No longer does that oval in the hand of the great Ascetic convey to the mind of one versed in symbolism the later signification which was attached to it; it, stands for the third eye of the Spirit, for that which is opened by Tapas, that which is opened within the brain of the ascetic when a certain stage has been reached, at which the lower forces are conquered for evermore. For the hand that forms the Cross stands as a symbol for that crucifixion of the passions of the lower nature by which only the Yogi may attain spiritual life; and the God who is the great Yogi has His uplifted hand in this position to show that every passion has been crucified, and so, by the crucifixion of the lower, the opening of the higher has become possible. Thus the Cross becomes the means of opening the door by which the light of the Spirit may stream out, and then comes the opening of the third eye, which is the Eye of Shiva, familiar to every Hindu in name if not in understanding. And that third eye - how did it show itself? Remember once more the ancient story that, as He sat engaged in Tapas, the Hindu God of Love strove to shoot his shafts at Him, but the forehead of Shiva opened, and from the third eye shot forth a ray of light which burned the tempting God to ashes. For when that eye is opened, none of the lower passions may venture to approach the ascetic who has achieved. And whenever, passing into the temple of the great God, you see him represented as the Maha-Yogi, then look you for the cord and realize its inner significance.

You may go a step further, and take to yourself the lesson that there is conveyed, that in man there is a power which may be used for the lower or for the higher life, either for the creation of new forms or for the evolution of spiritual life in man, but not for both; and therefore celibacy has been the note of the ascetic, a necessary preliminary before the third eye can be opened. Therefore always the idea of the ascetic includes this idea of absolute physical purity. Either you may drive the life current upwards towards Spirit, or you may drive it downwards towards Matter. If it seeks its expression in the material, it cannot at the same time rise up into the mightier creative energies of the spiritual sphere. And when Shiva upraises this Cross and cord which symbolize the opening of the third eye, it means that the life has been centred in the head, that the third eye of the ascetic has been opened, and by that centering at the higher pole the triumph of the Spirit is secured. You no longer have the downward tendency to Matter, you have achieved the triumph of the Spirit.

Let us seek the meaning of another symbol, in which Matter and Spirit are expressed, no longer divided but united. Here you have not the Cross and the oval but a double Triangle interlaced, showing that they are not to be separated, and so conveying to our thought the manifested universe and the union of Spirit and Matter in every possibility of phenomenal life. For here we have the Triangle upward pointing, which is fire or Spirit, and then the Triangle downward pointing, which is water or Matter, and the union of the two inseparable. This means the union of Spirit and Matter in the manifested universe; and the fact is that that union remains so long as manifestation endures. You will find this double Triangle used to symbolize two of the Hindu Gods, used as a symbol of Shiva, and used as a symbol of Vishnu; this is when these are regarded as two aspects of the One. The upward pointing aspect is taken as that of Mahadeva, that is fire; when He moves upon the waters, Narayana takes this symbol of the downward pointing Triangle to show the Deity evolving Matter, and so making phenomenal manifestation possible. So you again get the symbol of duality, in which you have the two Gods represented as one in Their essence, and only two in Their manifestation - fire and water, positive and negative, male and female, once again. That, to some of you, may throw light on an obscure suggestion that you may find in the Scriptures as to this inner relationship between the two great Gods of the Hindu faith.

Once more, in studying this, the story may come back to your mind that ought always to strike at the root of all bitterness between the modern sects - I use the word modern in comparison - who make the names of the Gods dividing walls, instead of uniting forces. For you may remember how a Shaivite worshipping in his temple felt a bitter hatred towards a neighbour that worshipped Vishnu, and worshipped, not in true religious spirit, but in antagonism to the other, whose chosen aspect of the God was different from his own. But lo! one day as he bowed before Mahadeva with the thought of anger in his heart against him who worshipped Vishnu, the image before him changed in aspect; it no longer stood there as Shiva only, but it divided in twain; one side remained in the form of Mahadeva, while the other side took the form of Vishnu, and the two together, no longer twain but one, smiled at the worshipper. If in modern times that story were understood, we should not see strife between two sects who worship one God under different aspects, and who should feel themselves as brothers, with no possibility of contention between them at all. And so studying these symbols, we come to the realization of the Divine in them, and to a clearer understanding of what underlies the outer form.

That leads me, following the same line of thought, to a more concrete kind of symbol. I take a concrete one on purpose, so that

19

I may trace it in its evolution and show to you how the abstract idea which is most congenial to the highly educated mind, gradually emerges from a symbol that is more concrete, a symbol necessary if religion is to be made intelligible to the unlearned and to the ignorant. Here you will permit me to say one word a little aside perhaps from the subject, but not aside from the controversies which are rending India today. There is no commoner attack made upon India in the West than what is called an attack on its idolatry, and you will constantly find bitter jeers and scoffs uttered by people who have been over here, who have seen idols and idol-worship, and ceremonies performed to the idol, but who have never understood them - nay, who have never taken the trouble to try and understand them, nor even to ask the worshipper what to him is conveyed by such doings. These visitors, looking at the outside with the prejudice engendered by foreign feelings, go back to their own land, and then from many a platform speak of the poor Indians as heathen, given over to idolatry, who ought to be taught a more spiritual religion, and rescued from this degradation that presses on their minds and hearts. Now this matter of idolatry is a very important one, because it turns on this most essential question - shall there or shall there not be accommodation to Ignorance? How may religion be made at once the teacher of the most degraded and also the object of reverence to the most highly instructed and the most aspiring minds? It is a hard problem to deal with, for that which is fit for the education of the ignorant is not fit for the philosopher and for the highly evolved thinker. The symbolism that teaches the one is repellent to the other, and if you are going to say that religion shall be exactly the same for one and all, then there are only two possibilities before you. If religion is to be one and the same for all, you must bring it to the limit of the very lowest intellect and of the least developed understanding; otherwise they will be shut out. If it is to be the same for all, the philosopher must come down to the level of the labourer or the child, and his noblest aspirations must find no grander vehicle than that which is capable of being grasped by the most thoughtless and the most uninstructed of the people. On the other hand, if religion is to be useful to all, then you must permit differences to come into it - differences of presentation, according to the mind that is to be met. You must have a religion philosophic for the philosopher and childish for the child - not because thereby you would drag down religion, but in order that you may lift up the childish mind, and train it for the possibility of future evolution, which may raise it to the greatest height of religious thought. Now in the West a different method has been adopted. In the West it has been attempted to make religion "so simple that a costermonger can understand it". In England that word implies, as a rule, the very lowest intellectual ability and training, a man in the street with a barrow, selling vegetables, who will be the representative of the outcaste amongst yourselves. I was once told that Theosophy can never be useful, because it is beyond the grasp of the costermonger. What has been the effect on religious thought in Europe of thus lowering the intellectual side of religion? Its effect has been that the intellect of the people has gone outside religion; you have a complete divorce between intellect and religion, and the greatest minds refuse any longer to accept a religion that outrages their highest aspirations, and in which they can find no food for lofty spiritual emotions. That is the price which is paid for the dragging down of the Divine Ideal, so that it may be grasped by the most ignorant mind.

In India you have the other plan. You have the recognition that men's minds are in different stages of evolution, that that which is true for the villager in his field is not true for the Brahman in his place of meditation. Both have rights in the religious world, and both have the possibility of the Spirit more or less evolved, therefore each should be fed with the food suitable for its evolution. You should no more feed the baby in intellect with the food of the man, than you should feed the baby in body with the food which is intended to support a man in his maturity. But that view means what is called idolatry; that means that you preserve the highest spirituality at the price of being misjudged by those who will not go underneath the outer sign of the idol. For the idol has different meanings according to the mind which the worshipper brings to it. The idol of the villager may be nothing more than some elemental form, to which he bows down, and to which he brings a drop of water or a flower, to which he strikes a bell. To the Brahman, worship of such a Deity would be degrading, but it means to that villager something that he is able to recognize and to worship; and the worshipping act on his part, the love and the faith that stir in him will open out the way for spiritual life. If you gave him the abstract thought of the Brahman, he would stand with open mouth, understanding nothing of its meaning; and you then would not stir in his heart the first faint throbbings of spiritual life. Let him have his idol which will be able to appeal to him, although it would be to you a degradation to worship it, and let the first quiver of spiritual life move within him. It will justify itself, it will begin his spiritual evolution, and, life after life, it will carry him onward to a higher, higher, and still higher view of Deity, until the Soul which began with the ringing of a bell before an Elemental shall find its home at the Lotus Feet of Mahadeva, lost in the radiance that ever flows therefrom. That is what becomes possible when you realize that the Soul is trained through many lives. If you have only one life and then for ever after what is called Heaven, you must hurry everything on: otherwise it is clear that when the Soul gets to Heaven it will find itself in a perfectly incomprehensible position.

In order to show you how this idolatry may be used, let me take, as I have taken elsewhere, an image that will be familiar to you: the image of Mahadeva on Nandi, His vehicle, the Bull. Now in a town when a day of festival comes, the image of the God is placed on this His vehicle, and is drawn through the streets of the town. It will be seen by many men whose minds are in different stages of evolution; to them it will convey different kinds of ideas. Let us first take the *Chhandogyopanishad* and the meanings which are given in that. Brahman is there spoken of as sitting on the Bull, but I take the more familiar form of Mahadeva on Nandi. What does it mean, taking it from the popular standpoint? I am now merely quoting. The sky is symbolized by the God, and the man who is called the theological worshipper will simply see the outer image of the over-arching sky, which to him is a most effective symbol of greatness and grandeur; for, than the sky which has in itself the sun, the moon and the stars - what more impressive symbol can you possibly have, what which would convey to the limited mind the idea of infinity, of the boundless life which fills all space? So to him, if he has been taught something at least of the meaning of symbols, the God will stand for the over-arching sky; and the Bull on which He rides will be the symbol of the world; and the four feet of the Bull, each of them having a special name, will tell him something of the way in which the world or the universe moves. For one foot will be Agni or fire, another foot will be Vayu or the God of wind - the Great Breath, in higher parlance, of the Supreme; another foot will be the Sun, as it shines, giving light to the world, and the fourth foot will be the quarters or the divisions of the sky. So to his mind these would be conveyed by this symbol, if someone would explain to him the idea of the over-arching care of the Divine, resting on the manifested world, and the sun, the fire, the wind and the quarters in the sky, all symbolized in these feet of the Bull that carry onward the God, and so support and guide the life of the manifested universe. Then some of you will seek after a subtler explanation that will be given you; and this is called the intellectual worship. Then the God will be the mind in man, and the God riding on His vehicle will be the mind dwelling in the body. Then the feet of the Bull will not have lost their significance, for one foot will be speech, another foot will be breath, another will be vision, and another will be the bearing. And then Shankaracharya teaches that as the four feet of the Bull carry the animal wherever it desires to go, so does mind attain its objects through speech, breath, vision and hearing, which bring the body and the Soul within it into contact with the outer and material universe. Thus by means of these feet of the Bull, the senses of the man, there may be carried inwards to the Soul the knowledge which the Soul has come into manifestation to seek. So you have your philosophic meaning of the idol as it passes through the streets, and it reminds you of the embodied Soul. And there is yet a deeper meaning that you will not find thus plainly given, but which you may work out for yourself or at least recognize when I give the explanation. Now let the God stand for the Divine itself, for the Spirit that we seek, for the highest manifestation - call It Brahman, call It Shiva, call It Vishnu, give It what name you will; but recognize the One, the All, the Indivisible, symbolized under this name and under this idol form. What then will mean the feet of the Bull? They will mean states of consciousness, whereby the Soul may climb upwards towards its Lord; so that foot after foot of the Bull shall be state after state of the Soul by which it comes nearer and nearer to the universal Spirit, until at last it shall find itself one with It. One foot will be the waking state in which the Soul lives and moves in its waking hours; the next foot will mean the Svapna state that we spoke of yesterday, which in the Soul is taken as a second step towards the Divine; the third foot will mean the Sushupti state, where one step more is taken towards the Divinity; and the last foot will mean the Turiya state, from which the Soul passes onward into unity with God. So that the loftiest conception of the spiritual Philosophy is brought to the developed mind when that symbol is seen. Thus I myself, familiar with this loftier view, constantly having that in mind, had it brought back to my outer consciousness with intensity and vividness, when walking through the temple of Madura, I saw an image, a sculptured form of the Sacred Bull, which became to my mind not a mere bull, carved in stone, but a voice that recalled the teaching that I had received of the states of consciousness, and reminded me of the upward path which ended in the God. Thus you may take what is called the idol and find in it what you bring to it; and if you have no spiritual life within you, which brings to it its real signification, you have no right to simply scoff at idolatry, which is empty to you only because you are empty.

So again you may take the *Puranas,* full of symbolism of the most complicated and difficult kind. If you want to understand how that symbolism may be explained, turn to a single question that you find dealt with in Madame Blavatsky's *Secret Doctrine*; and in the method of unravelling of one myth, you may possibly gain the key which may enable you to unlock for yourself many another mystery. I am only taking one out of a very large number of instances which she takes from the Pauranic stories, explaining their different meanings. The one that I select and to which I wish to draw your attention, and which I will not work out in detail, for you can read it for yourself, is that of the Maruts - the Gods of the wind and the children of Rudra, the Roarer, signifying the tones and the fore of the wind manifested in phenomenal shape. First of all that represents a fact in Nature. It represents the fact that behind every force in Nature there is an intelligence, that every natural phenomenon has an entity connected with it, so that in the plainest sense and the most obvious signification, these Maruts are entities that deal with certain forms of manifestation in the phenomenal universe; and if you understand them, their language and their powers, then the phenomena they control become subject to your knowledge. To no evolved spirit will the Maruts be objects of worship; they will be powers that he controls by his own will; no

Rishi would worship the Maruts, he would command them; but that does not alter the fact that they are real entities, that they have their real place in the Kosmos, that they are among the Devas, who are the spirit-side of every physical phenomenon that you see; and if you lose that fundamental truth of Occultism, and if in studying the physical phenomena you see the phenomena only and not the Spirit that controls, then you are simply blinding yourselves to the real lessons of Nature, and Matter has achieved over Spirit its last triumph, for not only does it conceal Spirit from physical vision, but also it conceals it from the Spirit that is in man. The Maruts then in their lowest signification are entities - entities connected with the atmospheric world, immediately connected with the production of winds and under subjection to the trained and purified will in man. Then there is another signification, in which you find them no longer as those entities in the Kosmos, but in their character as the children of Rudra - that Rudra who once more is Shiva and once more the Maha-Yogi. What then can be the signification of the children of the Yogi, the children of the Virgin Ascetic? They become then the passions of his nature, they symbolize the forces which he has mastered, and they become, from this standpoint, the enemies of man, striving at first against him; and then going higher, still keeping this symbolism of the ascetic, those which were his children of the lower nature, the passions that he had to conquer: they become the children of the higher nature, when the lower has been conquered by the purified will of the ascetic in which all power resides, and by them he may work in the external universe. Then you come to the story in which Indra tries to destroy them, for the child is to be born who is to destroy Indra himself, and Indra in this sense is the lower manifestation of Nature - the God of the sky, the bearer of the thunderbolt, symbolizing a manifested and physical Kosmos; and as the child to be born shall destroy him (once again, the Marut), Indra casts forth his thunderbolt, and in the womb he shivers the embryo into seven pieces, which again are divided seven-fold. It is the lower that has checked the development of the higher, and has turned into lower forma the forces that ought to have grown into the developed and purified will. And so, step by step, bringing together all the different symbols that you may find scattered through the *Puranas,* you will find that this conception of the Maruts may be translated into most instructive suggestions which may guide you in your own transmutation of your lower forces into higher, and the change of Kama, that physically creates, into a desire which in the Spirit is the source of all progress and the spring of all true life. I mention this particular case, because many of you may be inclined to study the matter - I ought not perhaps to say many - but if you desire to carry on the study further, you will find, if you will use this great teacher, H. P. Blavatsky, who was sent to us, as you ought to use her, that is, by studying the knowledge that she was given to convey to us, and using it as a clue to further knowledge, you may do for the world a service whose value it is impossible to estimate. You may take your own Scriptures with an accuracy of knowledge which she did not possess; you may take them in their original form in Sanskrit, a language that she had not mastered; and you may get from them in that language, the language of the Gods, using the light that she has placed in your hands, many an inner meaning and many a secret clue; then you may give these to the world and so carry on this work which she was sent here to begin and not to finish. For it is hoped by those who sent her that if a stimulus were given, there might be here and there a man amongst the Indian people who would spring forward to the light, and taking it from her hand would carry it onwards, and bring out of these ancient Scriptures a spiritual teaching, which is needed for the helping of the world. If there should be one man here who was inspired by this suggestion to study for himself, I should count it that her life had borne here its true fruit; for her reward would be really won only if an impulse were given to the spiritual life of the world.

And so I might take you through many another symbol, so I might point out to you many another thing. Let me take what appears so simple a case - a Brahman's thread. What does it symbolize? What ought it to represent? It symbolizes the triple nature of man, the lower, the middle and the higher; it symbolizes those three planes of consciousness of which I spoke yesterday; it symbolizes the three conditions of Atma, of which also I spoke; it symbolizes in addition to these the body, speech and mind. Take those signification, and then judge what it ought to mean when a man wears it. The world knows who wears it, and to eyes that are trained that outer symbol is either sanctified or desecrated according as it represents a reality or a lie. For first of all as regards body, speech and mind, it symbolizes the control of each; and therefore when the knots are tied in it, it means that the man who wears the thread has gained control over body, speech and mind. It conveys to the eye that sees it the idea of a man of perfect self-control, whose body can never betray him and whose senses can never conquer him; whose speech can never soil nor hurt one ear on which it falls, whose speech will he self-controlled, used only when there is something to be said which is worth saying, never used for an unkind word, for the Brahman is the friend of all creatures and his speech must always help and must never wound. And not only does it symbolize the man thus controlled in body and speech, but also it implies that control of the mind has been achieved, and that the mind is held by the grip of the triple cord with its knots upon it, so that it may serve as a helper to the highest that is in him, and be used for the service of men to whom the Brahman belongs. For the Brahman has no right of existence for himself; he lives for the people and not for himself. If he lives for himself he is not a true Brahman; he may have the outer signs of caste, he may have the triple cord, he may use the sacred name, and he may even obey the rules of his order; but these are only the outer shell. Only if he lives not for himself but for the world, is be of the Brahman caste, standing as the spiritual servant, which in the world he was to be. He came from the mouth of Brahma that he might be the spoken word of the divine life among men. That is the meaning of the Brahman. Whenever I see the thread, I think to myself whether it is a reality or not - does it represent a truth, or is it only the survival of an ancient custom which has become the worst of blasphemies? For the degradation of the highest to the lowest is the worst of degradations, it is the poisoning of the world, for it poisons the spiritual life in man. These words may seem strong, but they are of that spirit on which the ancient Scriptures are based. They are no stronger than Manu spoke; they are no stronger than may be found in such writings as the *Mahabharata*; they are no stronger than may be read in many a *Purana*; and if they seem a bitter irony today, as I know they do, it is because I am speaking the words of the old world in the modern world, and the contrast between theory and practice is too startling. Since, however, the theory is true, I, while still an outcaste, recognizing the fact, make no claim amongst you. I have none in my present condition, and I give outward recognition to that caste which ought to manifest the holiness of the Brahman. That is why I say that if India is to be regenerated, it must come from this caste that symbolizes her past, and therefore has in it the promise of her future, no matter what it may be today; that is why, when I am asked to initiate reforms, I answer: "Let me serve you with suggestion, with help, if you will, but let the leadership in reform belong to the spiritual caste which has the right of leadership, so that in coming it may come without destruction, without shivering the very foundation on which the future life of the people is to be builded."

I who say these things may seem to press unfairly on you, for you are not personally to blame that the whole land has fallen; you as individuals are a part of a great nation, and you with it have gone downwards. But what shall I say to you, my Brahman brothers, you whom I ought to be able to address as fathers? If I cannot do so, it is because I know in many things more than you do; I, an outcaste, who ought to sit at your feet as your pupil, cannot do so, because you have not the knowledge to give me which the pupil has a right to claim from the teacher if he bows down before him. I appeal to you, you of the spiritual caste, to uphold it, and to recognize its present degradation. And if I speak these words which seem to make a bitter contrast, it is because in your hands lies the spiritual future of these people, because though the whole nation has fallen and you have fallen with it, yet in you there is still the power that ought to be able to begin the upward path; and though success will only be by the toil of many generations, there is no reason why you should not begin today. I know too well that in a moment you cannot do it, and I know that for the time your cord must remain a mockery, and the nobler you are the bitterer the irony you will feel in wearing it, because you know what it represented and how it has fallen. I say that not in reproach, for who am I that I should reproach you? I say it in order that here and there amongst you a desire for higher life may be born, for I would send, even as by a thunderbolt, into your hearts the bitterness of the degradation, so that the possibility of rising upwards may be realized once more amongst men. For I would that each of you, feeling the degradation and recognizing it, should not cast off the sacred cord, but begin to purify the life and thus justify its wearing; and if only in small things a beginning were made, the first upward step would be taken. For there are many lives before us, life after life that stretches in front of you, a mighty caste not able now to live up to its glorious traditions. And therefore I say, let us take up the cup of our Karma, let us bear it onward bravely as brave men should bear, not quarrelling with its weight inasmuch as we have made it ourselves in the past; recognizing it as bitter, let us drink it, and in drinking it, let its bitterness purify the soul, that we may gain strength to change to all that we long for, and may be resolute to alter ourselves, and so the spiritual purification of the people also shall begin. Then when we come back to birth, as we shall come swiftly if our desire is to help the people to whom we belong, then we shall find things a little better, and in that better life we shall be able to work hand in hand when the triple cord will have lost the mockery between the wearing and the meaning, and so life after life we shall lift the whole of this people that has fallen in our fall, and will rise in our rise.

That is my last word to you in this hall, not a word of reproach but a word of common sorrow, and of common aspiration for this Hindu nation. We are responsible for it. Let us then begin the work of reformation, and from generation to generation we shall work until India shall rise step after step, and we shall place her again where she ought to be and where in truth she always is - at the feet of the Great Gods. Though the people do not see her there now, they shall see her there then; and then the light that springs from the Lotus Feet shall envelope her, so that the world shall worship her, and know that she is indeed the Spirit in the body of Humanity.

www.ingramcontent.com/pod-product-compliance
Lightning Source LLC
LaVergne TN
LVHW041503070426
835507LV00009B/797